Y0-EKS-090

celtic

MOUTH

MUSIC

cheek music chin music lilting diddlin [...] music purist singing jigging dowdling
diddlage reel a bouche turluttage kan [...] a beul cheek music chin music lilting

Mary Morrison, legendary singer of canntreachd, *with Mr. and Mrs. Furl Morrison, Barra, Scotland, 1953.*

For information or a catalog:
Ellipsis Arts...
P. O. Box 305
Roslyn, New York 11576
Phone: (516) 621-2727
Fax: (516) 621-2750
e-mail: elliarts@aol.com

CELTIC MOUTH MUSIC

EXECUTIVE PRODUCER
Jeffrey Charno

AUTHOR/PRODUCER
Matthew Kopka

EDITOR
Candace Ward

ALBUM SEQUENCE
Jonathan Pickow and Matthew Kopka

ART DIRECTOR
Joanna Jaeger

♻ Printed on recycled paper

A friendly visit, or ceilidh, *at home of Sarah Makem, Keady, County Armagh, 1953.*

CONTENTS

cheek music, chin music, lilting, diddling, gob-bing, pus music, purist singing, jigging, dowdl-ing, diddlage, reel à bouche, turlutage, kan ha diskan, port-a-beul, dandling —

—for all its names both beautiful and strange, mouth music's a very basic phenomenon. Built on favorite old melodies and rhythms, on the quips that slip out of folks when they're frisky or drunk, mouth music is for making music—especially for *dancing*—when there aren't instruments around. Though found in various forms throughout the world, mouth music is highly developed among the Gaels. The mesmerizing rhythms of mouth tunes made them a kind of Celtic street-corner soul music centuries ago, a tradition that has gained too little attention. Known as diddling, lilting, jigging and *port-a-beul* ("porsht-uh-bee-ul") in Great Britain and Ireland, mouth music became part of the musical baggage of Scots and Irish emigrants—driven abroad by poverty or persecution, and forced to travel light. It accompanied them to Newfoundland and Nova Scotia, where it was absorbed by Acadian and French-Canadian culture, and down into the southern Appalachians.

Beginnings

fal-al

"Mouth music" is likely a translation of the Scots Gaelic *port a beul* ("tunes from the mouth"), the genre's richest form. But whether from the mouths of practiced singers or tinkers, whether sung in English, Gaelic, the Doric of northeast Scotland or meaningless syllables, mouth tunes share certain irreducible traits: sexual frankness, delight in the absurd and—above all— the word-wizardry that propels their compound rhythms.

Though not all mouth music originates in dance (listen to Talitha MacKenzie's rendition of "The Cave of Gold," track 21 on the enclosed CD), it always *swings*. Sung with the sparse addition of bones, bells or jew's harps, if accompanied at all (in unison, traditionally, not harmony) mouth music continues to offer ground for experiment, and a reminder—in a time of increasingly sophisticated music production—of the power of the human voice.

fal-al da-diddle ay-do, fal-al da day

The most colorful story of Scottish mouth music's origin suggests it was born when the bagpipes were banned after the second Jacobite rising against the British crown in 1745. Nonsense lyrics were fitted to precious pipe tunes, helping players recall the intricate quavers that gave the originals "lift." The method ensured the classical body of bagpipe music was not lost. Mouth music, however, soon developed a life of its own, with practitioners contriving new tunes for dances, enlivening gatherings where instruments weren't to be found.

Like lots of good stories, this one smooths history's rough edges, and contains various contradictions. The bagpipes weren't ever banned, for one thing, though a man was hanged for possessing a set in York in the 1740s (disincentive enough!). A more complex memory system called *canntaireachd*, which bagpipers use to teach each other tunes, had long existed—and lilting a tune to teach the melody is a universal practice. Song and dance are also, of course, intimately connected; in some form, mouth music is undoubtedly ancient (the *gigue* form, on which much mouth music's propounded, has existed for over four hundred years). And mouth music, finally, has various precedents—Scots musical culture carries a wealth of imitative song forms, as Annie Johnston's exquisite bird songs on this album (track 25) demonstrate. Singing to accompany the rhythm of work activities, including rowing, reaping, spinning, milking and "waulking," or shrinking wool, is also a highly developed feature of Scottish culture.

Inishmore residents at gathering, Aran Islands, 1953.

ti yum tat ti

Scottish mouth music's greatest period of growth came during late nineteenth-century religious revivals, when Calvinist ministers forbade indigenous music. Church hostility to traditional pleasures—which sometimes saw violins, pipes and harps thrown onto bonfires—continued to this century.

Though the Catholic Church was also sometimes hostile to traditional music, Ireland's long periods of poverty are more central to mouth music's development there. In thousands of isolated villages well into the 1950s, lilting offered an opportunity to dance when the day's labors were done, and instruments—or musicians with sufficient skill and repertoire to keep the company dancing—were scarce.

The great singer Margaret Barry said Ireland's County Wexford was once "great country for diddling, or 'doodlin,' as they called it there." Paddy Tunney says "scrapy ould fiddlers were helped along" during Donegal dances by lilting from the crowd.* Singer and flute player Micho Russel of Clare says young women were "picked out specially" to lilt at weddings, often in groups of three—a pretty sight, one imagines, and a joyful noise.

"Everyone could lilt in them days," says 84-year-old fiddler and singer Tommy Gunn of his youth in Derrylin, County Fermanagh, Northern Ireland.

*Discipline and musical development are required to keep strict time for dancing. Gordon Easton of Aberdeenshire, Scotland, says that while a fair few people could conjure a tune on the melodeon or fiddle when he was young, "most couldn't play steadily enough for dancin', so they diddlt." Along the northeast coast, he says, they were often accompanied by "a comb and a bit o' paper."

ta ti diddle um

ti yum tat ti ta ti diddle

The good men and the good ministers . . . did away with the songs and stories, the music and the dancing, the sports and games that were perverting the minds and ruining the souls of the people, leading them to folly and stumbling . . . . [They] went among the people and brought them to forsake their follies and return to wisdom. They made the people break and burn their pipes and fiddles. If there was a foolish man here and there who demurred, the good ministers and the good elders themselves broke and burnt their instruments.

     Woman, Isle of Lewis, 1928, as reported in Alexander Carmichael's *Carmina Gadelica*.

Fiddler Johnny Hoare with neighbors, Lisbeemuir, West Cork, Ireland, 1953.

AN EARTHENWARE POT

In Derrylin there were these two fellows, the Gilroys. Tommy lilted, and Johnny was the best dancer you ever saw. They'd come out on the floor in the Owens' parlor—Tom, John and Mary, John's dancing partner, and Tommy would kinda get down on one knee. Then he'd start to lilt.

He'd start off nice and steady—*Doodle aiddle doodle aiddle doodle aiddle diddle dee dum . . .* and John and Mary would commence to dance a reel. John wore hob-nail boots, y'see, and Mary had a pair of clogs with steel strips 'round the bottom. Between the lilting and dancing it made a great sound.

Two of the Owenses were flute players; two were fiddlers—they hosted the country dances. None of them married anyone in his life. The only interest those people had was music—they'd play all night in order to get a tune right, and sometimes they woke the whole village fighting about how to play a reel.

I was only a young lad, fourteen or fifteen. One day a neighbor was making hay and went over to the Owens' for a rake—this is a gospel story I'm telling you. John Owens—he was one of the fiddle-playing Owenses—was digging a hole in the floor; he had dug up all the flagstones in the parlor! This fellow the neighbor looks down at John. "I'll tell you one thing, John," he says, "when you die they won't have to carry you far to bury you."

"Would you like to know what I'm doin'?" John asks. "Do you see that great earthenware pot outside? I'm gonna bury it here and put the flagstones over it. And when John and Mary dance, the rhythm'll be like a kettle drum 'neath their feet!"

Sure enough, it made an incredible sound. I used to lie in bed and listen to the music and dancing coming from the Owens' house. You could hear it all over the village, way out in the country . . .

TOMMY GUNN

Tommy Gunn demonstrates Johnny Gilroy's lilting style.

killy**ma**l**ing** killy**ma**-**lee** whiskey friskey

Tommy Gunn step-dances outside his home in County Fermanagh, Northern Ireland.

killy **ma-ling** killy **ma-loe** whiskey friskey

yum ti diddle-i diddle aido

cucunandy
cucunandy
cucunandy

cucunandy
cucunandy
cucunandy

yum t

Young woman performs at song contest in Cork, Ireland, 1940s.

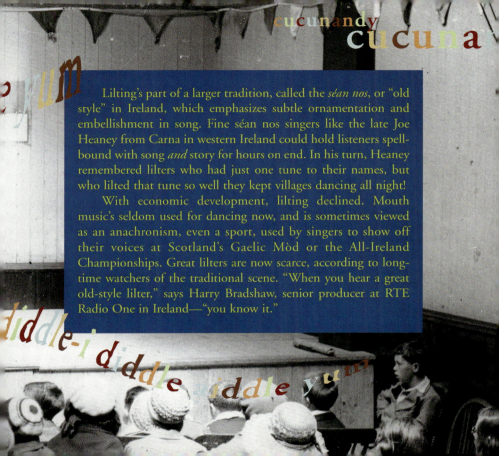

Lilting's part of a larger tradition, called the *séan nos*, or "old style" in Ireland, which emphasizes subtle ornamentation and embellishment in song. Fine séan nos singers like the late Joe Heaney from Carna in western Ireland could hold listeners spellbound with song *and* story for hours on end. In his turn, Heaney remembered lilters who had just one tune to their names, but who lilted that tune so well they kept villages dancing all night!

With economic development, lilting declined. Mouth music's seldom used for dancing now, and is sometimes viewed as an anachronism, even a sport, used by singers to show off their voices at Scotland's Gaelic Mòd or the All-Ireland Championships. Great lilters are now scarce, according to long-time watchers of the traditional scene. "When you hear a great old-style lilter," says Harry Bradshaw, senior producer at RTE Radio One in Ireland—"you know it."

A GLASS OF RUM PUNCH

There once was a man had three daughters. Their mother, God bless her, was dead. The father was the apple of his daughters' eye, they the apple of his.

One night the father came home sorta lame lookin'. He didn't feel good, and he went up to bed.

The daughters put their heads together. "What can we do to make daddy happy? We have to do something," they said. They decided to make him a glass of strong punch.

They got a big glass and filled it up with rum, adding cloves and hot water. They put sugar in it, and took it up to his bedroom and gave it to him.

The following morning their father was jumping on the landing! The oldest daughter came up and asked, "Did the rum do?"

"Did the rum do?" he laughed.

The second girl came up and asked, "Did the rum do, Da?"

"Did the rum do, indeed!" he laughed again.

The youngest came in and asked, "Did the rum do, daddy?"

Their father looked at them. He started to tap his foot and began to sing, *"Didderumdo, o didderumdo, o didderumdo dad-dy? Didderumdo, o didderumdo, o didderumdo, me daughters . . ."*

STORY OFTEN RECITED BY JOE HEANEY
(courtesy Ethnographic Archive, University of Washington)

Joe Heaney, séan nos *legend .*

CHAPTER 2

Puirt-a-beul

brochan lom,

> They have a great genius for music. . . . Several of both sexes have a quick vein of poesy, and in their language (which is very emphatic) they compose rhyme and verse, both of which powerfully affect the fancy.
>
> MARTIN MARTIN
> *A DESCRIPTION OF THE WESTERN ISLES OF SCOTLAND (CA. 1695)*

Puirt-a-beul singing is perhaps the most exquisite of mouth musics, a practice requiring rhythmic precision and Gaelic fluency. But despite the demands that such tunes make on singers, experts like Kenna Campbell insist puirt-a-beul aren't songs at all, but *instrumental* tunes whose lyrics power their rhythms.

"A Nova Scotian friend once proved this for me," says Campbell, "by chanting the words of some puirt-a-beul tunes without the music. My feet began to itch immediately—I couldn't help moving! The words are fitted so neatly for their rhythm, they perfectly match the steps of the dance. You really don't need the melody at all, we realized, the rhythm is held so securely by the words."

Great puirt-a-beul singing often travels in families. The Campbells hail from a long line of pipers from Greepe, on the Isle of Skye. "Most of the puirt we sing are also played on the pipes," says Campbell, whose two brothers, two sisters and two daughters are adept puirt singers like her father's family, from whom they learned the skill. "Our singing's strongly informed by the pipe's sound."

ana lom, brochan lom a subhan

brochan lom, tana lom

Kenna (left) and Mary Campbell—great puirt-a-beul singing travels in families.

As with other Celtic music, stringing together two or three puirt-a-beul in a satisfying set is an art in itself. "Ideally, you go for a related key in moving from one to the next," says Campbell. "But sometimes the *tessitura*—the combined range of pitch—is too wide. Then you must hunt for something else that works."

Occasionally, puirt-a-beul contain vocables (the "hollow" or nonsense syllables one finds in thousands of songs, which form the meat of lowlands Scots diddling and Irish lilts). Generally, however, they have lyrics, as in this song of Ewen's *coracle,* or boat, part of a class of puirt-a-beul probably devised for children:

> O look at Ewen's coracle
> With twenty-five white oars!
> Look at Ewen's coracle
> Passing the White Point.
>
> Ewen, Ewen
> Ewen will be skipper of her
> Ewen, Ewen
> Passing the White Point.

"It would be fascinating to know the circumstances in which these tunes arose, for the words are very clever," says Morag Macleod, a lecturer in Gaelic song at Edinburgh's School of Scottish Studies. "For the most part we don't know their origins or who made them." This translation of one, addressed to a fire that's slow to start, offers a hint of their whimsical qualities:

Ewen

Have you seen Oighrig? asked the spout, asked the spout.
Who was asking for her? asked the spout, asked the spout.
The hot one on the embers, said the spout.
Euphemia's own teapot! said the spout, said the spout.

"Quite a lot of them had bawdy texts," says Macleod. "When field historians first set out to collect them, people simply wouldn't sing them."

The meaning of many puirt-a-beul tunes is obscure. Some may have constituted a kind of insider speech. The lyric to one popular puirt-a-beul—"The ewe with the crooked horn has a full udder"—meant "the whiskey still is full," according to Macleod.

Great puirt-a-beul singing wants intensive practice. "Finding breathing spots is also an art," says Campbell, "something that must be worked out in advance." Often, such openings come nowhere near the end of a line, but in oxygen-affording hollows in the body of the tune. Listen to some of this album's puirt-a-beul singing (try programming tracks 10, 11, 13, 21, 24, 26 and 27 together) and you'll marvel at the singers' breath control.

You have to assume the music will be danced to, and sing with the absolute precision of instrumental music. You can't just break off and have a breath and a pie and a pint at the end of the phrase—if you do, someone's left with a leg up in the air!

KENNA CAMPBELL

Norman Kennedy

A Scotsman in Ireland

Once, while I was traveling through the Irish Gaeltacht—way back in the early '60s when the women were still wearing their shawls and the old men their *bainín* (the white homespun trousers made by local weavers), I stopped in a pub in a little coastal town called Spiddal. When the people learned I was a singer, they asked me to come home with them and give them some tunes.

We drove to a lonely farm out in the hills. We went inside, and there was an old woman seated by the fire. She had a rag in one hand and a snuffbox in the other.

They asked would I sing, and I replied that the custom, as I understood it, was a song from the host first, then singing till dawn from the guest. The old woman nodded; she appreciated my awareness. But she wouldn't begin unless the flute player held her hand—an old custom—to draw energy from him.

The first song that I sang was "Molly Bawn." Almost immediately the people began to shout, "My love on your voice!" and "Get it out well!" in Gaelic. When the Irish encourage you, you really get a boost. I took off!

I started to sing some mouth music, and they got excited. Stop, they said, stop! They hadn't heard that sort of music in thirty years. I waited while they laced up their heavy-studded boots, pulling their caps tight 'round their heads, then they made me start again. I sang for hours. Every time I stopped they cried *"Arís!"* ("Again!") They were step-dancing like fury—in the old style, their whole bodies moving on the flagstone floor. I tell you, the sparks really flew.

Norman Kennedy

"Let's Have a Couple of Sets!"

We'd get a bunch to gather of an evening, five or six fellers and three or four women, and they'd say, "Let's have a couple of sets!"

"Here," we'd say to one of the old fellows, "Go to work and give us a little cheek music." He'd sit down on the floor and haul his legs up and put his elbows on his knees and his chin on his hands, and sit and sing for hours.

BERTON YOUNG, WEST PETPESWICK, NOVA SCOTIA

Mouth music found new forms as it traveled to Europe and America, but it stayed close to the ground—that is, to dance. In the Canadian northeast (including logging camps where singer Allan Kelly, right, heard on track 28 worked as a sixteen year-old), *diddlage, reel à bouche, turlutage* or *chin music*, as mouth music was variously called, helped settlers retain their cultural moorings and do some step-dancing while they were at it. In the southern Appalachians, mouth tunes accompanied hoe-downs. Intricate foot-tapping, another wonderful traditional art, accompanies much Acadian and French-Canadian mouth music. And in Brittany, the thrice-repeated overlapping lines of *kan ha diskan* (or call-and-response singing) accompany vigorous stomping and movement.

"Lilting is the fastest way for a tune to travel from one imagination to another," says Paul MacDonald, a musician, producer and recording engineer from Cape Breton, Nova Scotia. "It's also a great way to pass the time while walking. As a young man, my friend Tommy Basker, who's now 73, often exchanged tunes with girls as they walked home from country dances, lilting as they went."

Mouth tunes proved infinitely adaptable. Sometimes, at least in Cape Breton, lyrics devised for puirt-a-beul turned back into accompanied songs. "By the turn of the century," MacDonald says, "Gaelic language use had waned. Many evenings the power was cut off, and there was little for people to do. So Tommy and his friends made up English words to the jigs and reels:

Mrs. McCarthy, give me your daughter.
No, no, no, I only have one.
She's gone out to fetch her water,
She'll be back when she is done.

"Of course, depending on the company," MacDonald allows, "there were alternate words:

Mrs. McGee went out to pee,
And I went out behind her.
She bent down to make her water
And I saw her old coffee grinder!"

Allan Kelly with friend at logging camp, circa 1919.

How Do You Diddle?

Lilters can become tight-lipped when asked for the keys to their art. "Some say there's a strict form, but it's just what comes natural," says Gordon Easton of Aberdeenshire, Scotland, who has for many years owned the diddling competition at contests in his part of the country.

Press Easton and he admits that diddling wants skill—skill he acquired in practice during years of solitary labor on his farm near the hill of Mormond, in the Blackhills of Tyrie. "Your mind has to be on the breathing more than the tune," says Easton—the reason why knowing an "air" intimately is a boon. When Easton diddles he employs variations long since worked out on the fiddle (he also plays "trump"—as the jew's harp is called in the northeast of Scotland—pennywhistle, "moothie"—harmonica—and melodeon).

One may diddle most any song (one may "dowdle" or "lilt" it as well, in the northeast, to lull a child), but "good gan" tunes as Easton calls them—reels, strathspeys, jigs, hornpipes, *schottisches* and other quick tunes—work best. For diddling competitions in the northeast, each singer performs a march, strathspey and reel.

Peter Kennedy, one of the fathers of the British folk revival and an accomplished mouth musician, advises new diddlers to "choose a tune you're intimate with, perhaps one known from childhood." Diddle it, Kennedy says, "as inventively as you can." Always, he notes, the aim is rhythm, or "lift."

Develop as many rhythmic variations as you can. Record the tune on a cassette player, comparing styles. "Work toward a single performance-quality version of your song," Kennedy advises. Take your show on the road.

One-man folk festival Gordon Easton (track 15) and his wife Isobel with advertisement for album containing Gordon's fiddle, jew's harp, harmonica and melodeon playing, diddling and singing.

Dolores Keane

1. **MRS. ARTHUR MACARTHUR**—". . . just a song you can dance to . . ." Outer Hebrides, Scotland, August 12, 1952. (0:10)

2. **AUDREY SAINT-COEUR**— *"Diddlage"*
Saint-Coeur is a member of a family of talented musicians and step-dancers, according to Lisa Ornstein, director of the Acadian Archive at the University of Maine. She has "spent most of her life on her parents' farm, leading a sheltered, somewhat reclusive existence, with music and song perhaps her most constant companions. Gifted with a phonographic memory, she has acquired a vast repertory of songs and tunes from her community and from listening to the radio." This tune, a quadrille (square dance) air, was recorded by ethnomusicologist Laurent Comeau in Néguac, New Brunswick, in 1976. (0:34)

3. **JOHN MACDONALD**—"Strathspey"/"The Reel of Tulloch"
"When I was a young lad, diddling was all the go in the northeast, ay an' in other parts of Scotland," John MacDonald told Peter Kennedy in 1935. "Away back in 1919, I competed in a diddling competition by a traveling concert party for the championship of Scotland, and I won it." MacDonald, who was born in 1905, was a mole catcher by trade, according to Kennedy. "He and his fellow catchers used to make moleskins into waistcoats. In addition, he repaired melodeons for all the plowlads in the northeast. At one stage he had a troupe with Jimmy McBeath that went around singing ballads and telling stories." MacDonald sometimes diddled with a goat bell and a rattle. (0:50)

4. **DOLORES KEANE AND JOHN FAULKNER**—"Mouth Music"
This song remains a favorite of Keane/Faulkner fans fifteen years after it was first recorded by the former husband and wife team. Keane is well known to

And now for "The Reel of Tulloch"!

fans of the Irish group De Danaan, with whom she has often sung. Multi-instrumentalist Faulkner was a member of the influential Critic's Group of Scottish singer-songwriter Ewan MacColl early in his career—MacColl used this tune as a warm-up vocal exercise. Fran Breen is the percussionist. (2:45)

5. **YANN-FÄNCH KEMENER**—"Marie Louise" (excerpt)
Yann-Fänch Kemener is among the most important figures of the Breton song revival. What music critic Stephen Winick calls Kemener's "weightless quality and gentle quaver" is evident in the slower passages of this beautiful example of *kan ha diskan* (call-and-response singing), in which Kemener is joined by diskaner Marcel Guillou. Sets of such tunes, created for the vigorous Breton dances, often last ten or fifteen minutes. The song tells of a young girl who dresses as a man and joins the army to be at her lover's side. Only on their return to the village, after nearly seven years, does she reveal her identity. Notice the way re-entry by each voice accelerates the rhythm of the song, which was recorded in 1977. (2:28)

The principle of *kan ha diskan* is simple: one of the executors, the *kaner,* reveals the first phrase. The second, or *diskaner,* sings the end of it with him, at least the very last notes, then repeats the entire phrase alone. The first singer joins him on the last notes, then continues the next phrase alone. Until the end of the song, each sings thus turn by turn, the ends of phrases being always said *à deux.* Whence a continuous unfolding, with a succession of reinforcements and diminutions of sound.

JEAN-MICHEL GUILCHER
Le tradition populaire de danse en Basse-Bretagne
(translation Stephen Winick)

John MacDonald

Francis McPeake, Jr.

6. BENOÎT BENOÎT—*"Reel à Bouche"*

The Acadian Ben Benoît's liltings, which appeared on the Archive de Folklore's recording *Acadie et Quebec,* became "a hit among us youngsters" in Montreal during the early 1970s, says singer André Marchand, who can be heard evoking the same tune on the track that follows (the tracks are segued together.) During the 1950s and '60s, Benoît, also a marvelous storyteller, proved an invaluable source for Luc Lacourcière, who founded the Archives and its huge collection of Acadian and French-Canadian folklore. Note Benoît's smooth toe-tapping. (1:05)

7. GREY LARSEN AND ANDRÉ MARCHAND—*"Reel à bouche acadien*—Horses, Geese, and One Old Man"

American singer and musician Larsen and Marchand create an elegant arrangement—almost a sonata—using Benoît's tune on this 1993 recording. Larsen sets up a drone on the harmonium and plays the flute solo; that's Marchand on feet, guitar and vocals. The recording was made in 1993. (04:16)

Nobody knows where the toe-tapping comes from. They make noise with their feet in Brittany, and folks have talked about a possible Native American influence. People ask and we don't really know, so we tell them that it's so cold in Quebec in wintertime, we have to tap our feet in order to stay warm!

ANDRÉ MARCHAND

8. THE McPEAKE FAMILY TRIO—"The Road to Ballynure"

The doleful harmonies of the McPeake Family Trio (father Francis and sons Francis and James) are unique, as was the family's musical combination of piping, rhythmic use of the harp and singing, which raised eyebrows when Peter Kennedy first introduced the group to folk audiences in the 1950s. Francis McPeake, Sr., born in 1885, authored several tunes that have become standards, including "The Wild Mountain Thyme." This song of love and travel adapts several motifs from "The Loughanure Tune," a performative work that combines *caoning* ("keening," or music sung over graves, sometimes by paid mourners), with storytelling and lilting. In the bittersweet original, a couple of boys pick up a man's lament at his wife's grave, turn it into a lilt and run off singing it. Fiddler Neil Boyle recorded this tune in Dunloe, County Donegal, Ireland, in 1953. Brother James plays the harp, his brother Francis the uillean pipes. (1:35)

As a youngster, back before the '14-'18 War, Francis McPeake was interested in Irish history, and received help from a local worthy who arranged for a blind piper named John O'Reilly to come from Galway to Belfast to teach him the pipes. O'Reilly arrived with a label around his neck that said that he was to go to McPeake. McPeake had him at his house for only two weeks, and he learned the pipes. For many years McPeake was the only uillean piper in Belfast.

PETER KENNEDY

9. **BRIDGIT FITZGERALD**—*"An Sean duine dóite"* ("The Burnt Old Man")
Lilting is often distinct—softer, like its name, than diddling or puirt-a-beul. In this song, whose chorus is lilted, the speaker regrets marrying an old man. She's stuck him in a corner, the lyrics say, with *"just enough sour milk and a bit of barley bread. If he sticks his head out, I'll cut off his nose!"* Fitzgerald, a founding member of the Irish-American group Cherish the Ladies, was born in Inverin, Galway, in Ireland's Irish-speaking *Gaeltacht*. Her uncle Johnny Coyne taught her and her brothers and sisters to dance by lilting for them.(1:27)

10. **KENNA AND MARY CAMPBELL**— *"B'fhèarr mar a bha mi 'n uiridh/Fear an Dùin Mhóir"* ("Horo! My Regret"/"The Lord of Dunmore")
These tunes are part of a large body of puirt acquired over the years by the Campbell family, originally from Greepe on Scotland's Isle of Skye. Sisters Kenna and Mary recorded them in 1968 in Glasgow, where they were both schoolteachers; Kenna's daughter Mary Ann (track 27) was then six weeks old. Kenna is leader of the group Bannal, which preserves another great Scottish musical tradition, that of *waulking* songs, the songs that accompany the fulling of tweed. *"Better the way I was last year,"* the first tune goes, *"Than what I am come to this year. Better the way I was last year, when men came asking for me. O! Horo! my regret I'm not again a maiden."* The Laird of Dunmore's courting Marion, the speaker in the second tune announces, *"But who will court poor Mary?"* (0:59)

11. **NORMAN KENNEDY**—"Puirt-a-beul"
Kennedy was born in Aberdeen, Scotland, and lived for a time across the street from the great northeast singer Jeannie Robertson (track 29). At nineteen he went to Barra in the Hebrides, to study weaving (he is now a master weaver). In Barra he met another important figure, Annie Johnston (see track 25) and began learning Scotland's west coast singing style from her. According to Kennedy, Johnston made him do a chore for each song she taught him—a weaving song was earned by ironing sheets. He learned in the old manner, by memory, slowly absorbing countless songs, stories and other details "of the old life." Kennedy, who made this recording in 1965, now lives in Vermont, and teaches and concertizes throughout the U.S., Canada and Scotland. (2:05)

12. COLM O'DONNELL—"Molly Brannigan"

O'Donnell, a Sligo farmer (he lives in Monalea, high in Ireland's Ox mountains, where he breeds sheep), has won the Irish lilting championship in every age group—under 12, under 15, 18 and in the senior class. He succeeded both his father and brother (both of whom are named Seamus) to the lilting title. O'Donnell also plays flute, button accordion and fiddle. He'd never sung this tune "before *or* since," he says, and held the lyrics before him while he performed it for this 1993 recording. In addition to first-class lilting, O'Donnell employs some very jazzy syllables in his refrains. (2:07)

13. EILIDH MACKENZIE—"Puirt-a-beul"

Born on the island of Lewis in Scotland, Eilidh Mackenzie has taught traditional song and language in Nova Scotia and on Prince Edward Island in Canada, and was part of the Scottish group Mac-Talla, along with Christine Primrose (track 24). A clever drum arrangement links these four tunes from Mackenzie's first album, made in 1992. The extraordinary rhythms are supplied by world champion Scottish pipe-band drummer Jim Kilpatrick; unison singing and occasional harmonies are by Eilidh's sister Gillian. (2:40)

14. TOMMY GUNN—"Lilting with Fiddle, Guitar and Bones"

"Tommy is one of the great carriers of the Irish tradition," says Temple Records' owner and producer Robin Morton, who first met Gunn when he was running the folk club at Queens University in Belfast, in 1963. "(Gaelic singer) Harry Oprey told me that there was a great fiddler living just around the corner. I went and introduced myself." Gunn became both a friend to and abiding inspiration

for Morton's band, The Boys of the Lough. "Tommy's an immense talent who never got the recognition he deserved," Morton says. "He never really pushed himself. He always said, 'I'm a traditional man,' and it was true. He played in a very County Fermanagh style. All the most popular tunes of the early Boys of the Lough—'The Nine Points of Roguery,' 'Lady Anne Montgomery' and many others that became popular in the sessions—all came from Tommy." This track, from a 1980 session, features Tommy on bones, his son Brendan on fiddle, and Jim O'Halloran on guitar. (0:51)

15. GORDON EASTON—"The Drunken Piper"

Easton kicks off this march in a deceptively simple manner, setting out the melody and introducing changes in the crisp northeast Scots fiddle style. Each new decoration is a minimalist delight, with Easton's artistry becoming more apparent as he progresses. Easton has won many prizes for his mouth music in northeast competitions. "It's been fun, but my diddlin' days are comin' to an end," he reports. He's still in great form, however, on this 1995 recording. (0:41)

Up here in the northeast, they used tae supply the fiddle and melodeon players wi' a dram o' whisky to get the best oot o' them for the entertainment. The bottle wis put on a table, the glass set aside it, and "help yourself." But—the greedy divils—help themselves they did! They had to get someone to diddle and keep the music going till they revived. GORDON EASTON

16. JOSIE McDERMOTT—"The Collier's Reel"

The late McDermott was "a true bard," according to Robin Morton. A Sligo man like Colm O'Donnell, McDermott wrote many songs, and was Irish champion on

Josie McDermott

the whistle, alto saxophone, flute, and as a lilter. McDermott, who loved all kinds of music, including jazz, sings with casual mastery on this track, produced by Morton in 1976. (0:59)

17. TIM LYONS—"Within a Mile of Dublin"

Lyons, a one-time member of the group De Danaan, is one of Ireland's great accordionists, and the influence of his squeezebox-mastery can be heard in his lilting. He studied the singing of both Paddy Tunney and Joe Heaney, but his style is unique. That's banjoist Charlie Piggot checking in briefly with the D drone on banjo on this recording, made during a De Danaan concert in Washington, D. C., in 1978. (1:30)

18. PADDY TUNNEY—"Scots Bagpipe Lilts"

This style of lilting, far removed from strict Gaelic *canntaireachd* (the method by which Scottish pipers teach each other tunes) is sometimes called "cantering" by singers. Tunney, reportedly still going strong at 75, was a member of the Irish Republican Army in the early 1940s, and did five years in the Belfast jail for carrying explosives; he reportedly exchanged jigs and reels with fellow prisoners by tapping on the water pipe in his cell. Tunney often lilted for dances, sometimes with fiddlers, flute players and melodeon players accompanying. Notice how he carries his "piping" to its logical conclusion, squeezing out the "bladder" at the end of the tune, which was recorded in 1952. (0:59)

When we first began to produce the BBC Sunday Morning folk music series "As I Roved Out," we had a letter from Paddy Tunney, written from the jailhouse in Belfast. He was chiefly a poet then—it was quite normal in those days to be writing poetry and planting bombs—but while he was in prison he had begun to

Paddy Tunney

Elizabeth Cronin

remember many of the songs that his mother Brigid had taught him. He introduced us to his mother, his two sisters, his brother, and his uncle Mick, every one of them a fine singer, and we recorded them all.

PETER KENNEDY

19. **JOE HOLMES AND LEN GRAHAM**—"The Girl That Broke My Heart"
Holmes and Graham each ornament this tune in slightly different fashion—the result is a sort of glorious heterophony. Robin Morton, who produced the track, says the style arose spontaneously in the studio. Holmes, a fine traditional singer and fiddler from County Antrim in Northern Ireland (like Graham), died a few weeks after this recording was made in 1977. Two All-Ireland fiddlers played laments at his funeral and graveside. (1:42)

20. **ELIZABETH WHITE**—"Piping Imitation"
Appalachian folk singer and folklorist Jean Ritchie and her husband, photographer George Pickow, made these recordings of Betsy White of Fraserburgh, Aberdeenshire, Scotland, in 1953. Their guide was Hamish Henderson of the School of Scottish Studies. "Henderson knew what was needed to set everyone's throat at ease—the bowl went around," says Ritchie, and soon everyone was "quite happy." White *is* in good fettle here, performing these brilliant pipe imitations and a rhyming toast to a mythical Betty Campbell. (1:02)

21. **TALITHA MACKENZIE**—*"Uamh an Oir"* ("The Cave of Gold")
The Gaels divide instrumental music into three categories: *ceòl beag, ceòl meadhanach,* and *ceòl mór,* and there are examples of puirt-a-beul in each of these. The vocalized dance tunes heard on the rest of this album fall into the first category;

pìobaireachd tunes like the famous *"Cha till MacCruimean"* are examples of the latter. *"Uamh an Oir,"* according to Gaelic scholar John MacInnes of the School of Scottish Studies, lies in the middle category. The song tells the story of a piper who enters a cave, only to be ensnared by a supernatural being. From deep in the cave comes his cry—*"Oh that I had three hands, two for the pipes and one for my sword!"* Note the stylized pipe imitation in the chorus; the pipe drone was supplied by James MacDonald Reid. (2:10)

22. **ELIZABETH CRONIN**—"The Little Pack of Tailors"
Jean Ritchie and George Pickow collected this and some 50 other tunes by Cork singer Bess Cronin (see photo, previous page) during their visit to Ireland in 1952. The recordings had considerable impact—Cronin's quiet style inspired many revival singers, and "The Little Pack of Tailors," which is sometimes deployed as a "dandling" song by Irish mothers to bounce babies, has since been performed by many artists, including Len Graham. Cronin died in 1956. (1:00)

23. **SEAMUS ENNIS**—"What Would You Do?"
Ennis was with the intrepid musicologist Alan Lomax when he (like Jean Ritchie and George Pickow before him) visited Cronin (previous track), and adapted lyrics he had learned from her for this song, a working woman's take on the harshness and absurdity of existence. Pickow and Ritchie recorded Ennis in London in 1953. (1:40)

24. **CHRISTINE PRIMROSE**—*"Tha m'Inntin raoir"/"A'Mhisg a Chuir An Nollaig Oirnn"* ("Last Night My Mind Was. . ."/"The Drunkenness That Christmas Brought Us")
Christine Primrose, a native of the Island of Lewis in Scotland's Outer Hebrides,

Seamus Ennis and Jean Ritchie

Annie Johnston

is a thoroughly modern woman who sees no paradox between her love of the blues and other popular music, and the ancient songs of her ancestors. Long study of Gaelic singing has enabled Primrose to arrive at something that is both contemporary and that honors the tradition. Of these tunes and how she came to put them together, she says, "It's just a wee thing that satisfies me." (2:04)

25. **ANNIE JOHNSTON**—"Bird Imitations" (Mouth Art)
Each of these jewels of mouth art sketches the briefest of stories in the voice of a bird. The birds include—as edited here—a grouse, a black-backed and an ordinary gull, a crow, a rook, a chicken, a puffin, a razorbill, some thrushes and a seagull. "Lie down, sleep," the grouse tells her young, "You won't get any more food until the morning." The crow sings to the crab—"Come out while I shape a red coat for you!" eager to dash the crustacean against the rocks, and get at its meaty insides. "I've laid two eggs!" the rook brags. "I lay two eggs every day," the chicken retorts. The puffin and razorbill are enticing their young to fly. "Here I am at the edge of the sea," says one bird, "And I can't swim a stroke!" A schoolteacher, Annie Johnston worked with many scholars, helping document Hebridean traditions from the 1950s through the 1970s. This recording was made on Barra by Alan Lomax in 1951. (1:24)

26. **FINLAY MACLEAN**—"Puirt Medley"
Maclean, a fireman from the Isle of Harris, Scotland, was a member of a marching band that George Pickow and Jean Ritchie saw passing down a street in Inverness one day in the spring of 1953. They fell in behind the drummer, and at parade's end persuaded some of the musicians to join them for a drink. Later they recorded Maclean, the fiddler, performing these tunes. (1:59)

27. **MARY ANN KENNEDY**—*"Dh'fhalbhainn sgiobalta/Meal do bhrogan/Nead na lach' as a luachair"* ("I Would Go Quickly"/"Enjoy Your Shoes"/"Ducks' Nest in the Rushes")

Mary Ann Kennedy is Kenna Campbell's daughter (see track 10). Classically trained at the Royal Scottish Academy of Music and Drama, she is a master musician on both the concert harp and the *clarsach,* the Scottish small harp, and has also won prizes for her piano playing. In addition, she is a TV and radio host for the BBC, Scotland. Her youthful voice is quite irresistible here. (3:13)

28. **ALLAN KELLY**—*"La cou de ma bouteille"* ("My Bottle's Neck")

Allan Kelly (pictured on page 25) was born in an Acadian village in New Brunswick, Canada, in 1903, of Scots-Irish and Acadian descent, and married a French-speaking woman. Such relationships epitomize the closeness of the Irish and French musical traditions in the Maritime Provinces. Like many, Kelly and his family suffered incredible poverty in the early decades of the century, when the lands in the interior of New Brunswick were still being settled. According to Ronald Labelle of Moncton University's Acadian Studies Center, the high illiteracy rate in northern New Brunswick helped keep oral traditions in the region alive. This drinking song, recorded in December 1993, was popular throughout French Canada, and has been found as far away as Louisiana. (1:04)

29. **JEANNIE ROBERTSON**—"The Cuckoo's Nest"

"Ethnomusicologist and singer Hamish Henderson was the person who discovered Robertson, going around to tinker camps. He managed to get her awarded an M.B.E. (a distinguished service order from the Queen)," says Peter Kennedy. "I recorded this song, a very popular hornpipe, in 1953, just as Jeannie began to remember all sorts of children's rhymes. She was just at that point of remembering way back to her childhood, and it was pouring out of her. This was before she began going round to folk clubs and became famous. Robertson, who lived from 1908 to 1975, was a traveling person—she was actually born in the fields." (0:42)

30. THE GOADEC SISTERS—*"La poule qui couve"* ("The Hen That Lays")

Eugénie, Maryvonne and Anastasie Goadec inspired many singers when they first came on the Breton scene in the 1960s. Championed by Breton harpist Alan Stivell, they delighted all who heard them with their enormous repertoire of songs, learned from their grandmothers, parents, aunts and (in the case of this song) neighbors. The eldest sister was 75 when this song was recorded in 1975. Eugénie, the sole survivor, now sings with her daughter, Louise Ebrel. *"It was on an island in the sea,"* the lyrics to this song say, *"that I placed my hen to lay . . . I obtained seventeen eggs and eighteen chicks!"* (1:13)

31. SARAH MAKEM—"As I Roved Out"

Sarah, mother of singer Tommy Makem, was visited by Jean Ritchie and George Pickow in Keady, County Armagh, Ireland, in 1953. "She immediately invited us to tea," recalls Ritchie. "She was humming and singing 'As I Roved Out' while she got dinner—a lovely thing we asked her to record. She sang for us awhile, then we asked if she knew any other singers. 'Why don't I just invite them to the house tonight?' she said. She went to all the shops to spread the word, and we had a party (see photo, page 58). That evening, Sarah's son Tommy (upper right corner of photo, page 3), who was about seventeen, played the tin whistle for us. At the time he knew only one tune, but he got interested in the old songs as a result of our visit. After that, we learned that he went around to the neighbors saying 'sing

Jeannie Robertson

me all the songs you know.' So we feel slightly responsible for the illustrious career he went on to have with the Clancy Brothers!" (0:53)

32. **LES CHARBONNIERS DE L'ENFER**—*"La luette en colère"* ("The Angry Uvula")
"Hell's Coalmen," as this group calls itself, may be doing more to advance mouth music tradition than anyone else. The Quebecois group got its start when singer/composer Michel Faubert gathered present members Michel Bordeleau, Normand Miron, Jean-Claude Mirandette and André Marchand to create some lilting for an album. "We gathered around a table and started to sing," says Marchand. "We enjoyed it so much, we decided to keep going." The number of voices and occasional harmonies employed in the group's arrangements, Marchand acknowledges, is not traditional. "It's instinctive and fun, not a cerebral thing. We never talk about whether we're doing something special—our sound is 98 percent accidents!" (1:56)

33. **JEAN REDFORD**—"Children's Songs in Lallans Scots"
These songs, some of which may have been translated into *Lallans* (Lowland Scots) by Robert Burns, demonstrate how words function in mouth music, emphasizing the rhythm of the tune. Redford, a retired schoolteacher from Banffshire in the northeast, was recorded for this album by singer Tom McKean. (1:10)

> We wint tae bed tae rest at ease,
> And somebody happened tae gie a sneeze,
> That wauken'd half a million fleas
> In the lodgin hoose at Rothesay-o.

Refrain:	Dirrum a dee a doo a day,
	Dirrum a doo a daddie-o
	Dirrum a dee a doo a day,
	The day we went tae Rothesay-o.

Some o the fleas were big as bugs,
An' some were big as terrier dugs,
They sat on the bed an' they cockit their lugs
In the lodgin hoose in Rothesay-o.

34. PADDY DORAN—"The Roving Journeyman"

"Paddy Doran was a tinker, or traveling person, from County Waterford, one of a number of such people I recorded with Sean O'Boyle in Belfast in 1952," says Peter Kennedy. "We recorded them just on the outskirts of the city. A whole lot of tinkers were there, all these old barrel wagons drawn up right in front of this modern 1930s housing estate; we recorded songs and mouth music through the night. The following year, I went to find Doran and he was in jail—he'd been accused of stealing aluminum, and they wouldn't let me record him." (1:09)

In the early part of the century there was an itinerant who roamed along the border towns and villages from Dundalk, past Crossmaglen, Camlough, Carrickmacross and on to Redhills and Ballyconnell, accompanied by a tame bear that he led with a chain. The bear could do a spot of step-dancing, and by way of accompaniment the itinerant lilted, not untunefully either, this little stanza: *Da rum die daddy di rum do. . . .*

W. D. MURROW, reporter, *The Belfast Telegraph*

35. **FRANK QUINN**—"The Four Courts Reel" (excerpt)
According to ethnomusicologist Philippe Varlet, who introduced us to this recording, "Quinn was an Irish-born New York policeman and an all-round entertainer who could play fiddle and sing at the same time. As far as I can tell, this is the longest section of Irish lilting on a 78-rpm record." Quinn unleashes cascades of stunning triplets, accompanying himself on accordion in this song. The 78 was issued by Gennett Records, which produced a number of ethnic records in the early 1920s (by, among others, Jelly Roll Morton). It was made in New York City in February 1924. (2:51)

36. **MADAME BOLDUC**—*"Mon vieux est jaloux"* ("My Old Man's Jealous")
Bolduc (née Mary Travers, of Irish and French descent) was Quebec's first commercial singer-songwriter of note. Her topical, humorous songs held enormous appeal for the Quebec working class and rural people who flocked to Montreal in search of work during the early decades of this century. Bolduc, whose career was cut short by cancer in 1941, piloted her own plane to concerts throughout North America, dropping flyers advertising her appearances on towns where she was to play. Her most famous song, "Ça va venir" ("It Will Come"), exhorted listeners to keep faith during the Depression's hard times. Bolduc played harmonica and fiddle; on this recording, issued on a 78 record in 1930, she can be heard playing harmonica and jew's harp; her daughter Denise, who died in 1995, plays piano. (2:50)

37. **EMMA SHELTON**—"Pretty Little Girl with a Blue Dress On"
Maud Karpeles—the British collector who recorded this song—noted that jigs like it were "often sung as ditties on their own account, but their primary purpose

My old man's jealous!

was to accompany step-dances (hoe-downs)." A number of stock phrases might be fitted to the rhythm of the tune; commonly diddled tunes included "Skip to My Lou," "Cindy," "Shortnin' Bread" and "Black-Eyed Susie." American southerners applied the term "mouth music" to various musical and extra-musical phenomena, including hollering, barking, cheering and counting off. Diddling for dancing was considered less "devil-oriented" than playing an instrument such as a fiddle, according to Karpeles. Shelton lived in Carmen, North Carolina; Karpeles recorded her in Flagpond, Tennessee, in September 1950. (1:07)

When my Aunt Maud Karpeles went to the United States, she and her collaborator were taken for German spies—people thought it was strange that they should be going around collecting ballads in the middle of a war. They went to places that were very hard to get to, climbing up mountains and through dried-up river valleys, sometimes with a mule. . . .

PETER KENNEDY

(Total running time: 66:43)

Madame Bolduc; daughter Denise is co-pilot.

TRACK CREDITS

1. from the Helen Dunlop Collection, ARCHIVES OF TRADITIONAL MUSIC, Indiana University
2. from the collection of Johanne Larochelle, *DIVISION DES ARCHIVES ACADIENNES*, Laval University, Canada. Trad. Arr. Audrey Saint-Coeur
3. from *Mouth Music of Britain and Ireland*, FOLKTRAX 30, Trad. Arr. John MacDonald
4. from *Dolores Keane*, ROUND TOWER RECORDS 1, RTMCD1
5. from *Chants profonds de Bretagne, vol. 1: Kanou Kalon-Vreizh*, ARION ARN 64167. Trad. Arr. Yan-Fänch Kemener
6. from the Luc Lacourcière Collection, Archives #8717, *DIVISION DES ARCHIVES ACA-DIENNES*, Laval University, Canada. Trad. Arr. Benoît Benoît
7. from *The Orange Tree: Irish and French-Canadian Roots*, SUGAR HILL SH-CD-1136. *"Reel à bouche acadien"* Trad. Arr. Grey Larsen and André Marchand, "Horses, Geese, and One Old Man" by Grey Larsen, Pub. 1993 by Sleepy Creek Music
8. from *The Jug of Punch*, FOLKTRAX 071. Trad. Arr. The McPeake Family Trio
9. recorded for this album. Trad. Arr. Bridgit Fitzgerald
10. Kenna Campbell. Trad. Arr. Kenna Campbell
11. from *Ballads and Songs of Scotland*, FOLK-LEGACY RECORDS, INC. FSS-34. Trad. Arr. Norman Kennedy,
12. from *The Sound of Coleman Country*, COLEMAN HERITAGE CENTRE, Gurteen, Co. Sligo CD CC001. Trad. Arr. Colm O'Donnell, Pub. Coleman Heritage Centre
13. from *Eideadh Na Sgeulachd*, TEMPLE COMD2048/CTP048. Trad. Arr. Eilidh Mackenzie, Pub. Kinmor Music
14. Trad. Arr. Tommy Gunn
15. recorded for this album. Trad. Arr. Gordon Easton
16. from *Darby's Farewell*, TOPIC 12TS 325 (1978). Trad. Arr. Josie McDermott, Pub. Kinmor Music, soon to be re-released by TEMPLE RECORDS
17. Trad. Arr. Tim Lyons (engineering, Jesse Winch)
18. from *Mouth Music of Britain and Ireland*, FOLKTRAX 30. Trad. Arr. Paddy Tunney

19. from *After Dawning*, TOPIC 12TS401 (1979). Trad. Arr. Joe Holmes/Len Graham, Pub. Kinmor Music, soon to be re-released by Temple Records

20. from THE RITCHIE/PICKOW COLLECTION, Trad. Arr. Elizabeth White, 1996

21. recorded for this album. Trad. Arr. Talitha MacKenzie. Talitha MacKenzie appears courtesy of SHANACHIE ENTERTAINMENT CORP. A complete version of this song appears on the album *Solas*, 7908 Shanachie Records in the U.S., and on Riverboat Records, U.K. TUG 1007.

22. from THE RITCHIE/PICKOW COLLECTION, Trad. Arr. Elizabeth Cronin, 1971

23. from THE RITCHIE/PICKOW COLLECTION,. Trad. Arr. Seamus Ennis, 1971

24. recorded for this album. Trad Arr. Christine Primrose, Pub. Kinmor Music

25. from *Mouth Music of Britain and Ireland*, FOLKTRAX 30, Trad. Arr.. Annie Johnston

26. from THE RITCHIE/PICKOW COLLECTION, Trad. Arr. Finlay Maclean, 1996

27. from *Strings Attached*, MACMEANMNA RECORDS, SKYECD 05. Trad. Arr. Mary Ann Kennedy, Pub. Macmeanmna MCPS, Quay Brae, Portree, Isle of Skye, Scotland IV51 9DB. Recorded at Temple Recording Studio, Midlothian, Scotland. c & p Macmeanmna 1991. All rights reserved.

28. from *Suivant l'étoile du nord*, *LE CENTRE D'ÉTUDES ACADIENNES*, University of Moncton, WRC1-4131, New Brunswick, Canada. Trad. Arr. Allan Kelly

29. from *Mouth Music of Britain and Ireland*, FOLKTRAX 30, Trad. Arr. Jeannie Robertson

30. from *The Goadec Sisters, KELTIA MUSIQUE* KMCD 11. Trad. Arr. The Goadec Sisters

31. from THE RITCHIE/PICKOW COLLECTION, Trad. Arr. Sarah Makem, 1965

32. from *Chansons a cappella*, LES CHARBONNIERS DE L'ENFER. Trad. Arr. Les Charbonniers de l'Enfer, SOCAN 1996

33. recorded for this album. Trad. Arr. Jean Redford

34. from THE RITCHIE/PICKOW COLLECTION, Trad. Arr. Paddy Doran

37. from FOLKTRAX 907. Dr. Maud Karpeles, *Appalachian Collection, North Carolina and Tennessee*

Mastering by Jonathan Pickow, Greenhays Studio, Port Washington, NY
Additional mastering by Pacific Coast Soundworks, West Hollywood, CA

Everyone gathers for farewell photo after evening at Sarah Makem's, Keady, County Armagh, December 1953. That's Jean Ritchie and Sarah on left, third row.

My father's aunt Lizzie came to live with us when I was born. She was a first-class lilter and a great source for Gaelic songs. She often corrected her brothers (all four of whom were fiddlers) and other local musicians on their settings of the old tunes.

The first years of my life were difficult because I had asthma, and because I was home a lot Lizzie and I became very close. I used to get up early and find her in the corner of the kitchen, knitting and gently lilting in her rocking chair. I'd climb up onto her lap, curl up there, and rock the chair to the rhythm of her lilting. It became our morning ritual, and lasted all through my childhood. I'll always remember the morning when I got up and she wasn't there.

PAUL MACDONALD

When the "praties are dug and the kettle boils over..."
Inishmore, Aran Islands, 1952.

R E S O U R C E   G U I D E

*Bannal's waulking songs and the School of Scottish Studies Scottish Tradition series (including *Calum and Annie Johnston* and *Bothy Ballads)* are available from Greentrax Records, 3 Morven Street, Edinburgh, Scotland EH4 7LG

*The music of *Les Charbonniers de l'Enfer* is available from Thirty Below, in Quebec City, Canada. Call (418) 847-9815 for a catalog

*Folk Legacy Records' address is: Sharon, CT 06069. Tel. (860) 364-5661

*for a catalog of great music from around the world, write Folktrax Records, 16 Brunswick Square, Gloucester, England GL1 1UG, or fax 44 (01) 1452 503 643

*Listen to *From Galway to Dublin: The 78 Era*, on Rounder Records

*for more of the music of Sarah Makem, Elizabeth Cronin and others, write Greenhays Recordings, 7A Locust Avenue, Port Washington, NY 11050

*Keltia Musique is distributed in the United States by Allegro

*Norman Kennedy's recording *Songs and Stories of the Old People* is available from Golden Fleece Publications. Call 1 (800) 232-5648.

*Shanachie Records has great folk! Call (201) 445-5561 for a catalog.

*for more great northeast Scots music, check out *Singin is Ma Life,* by Jane Turriff, on Spring Thyme Records. For a catalog write to the company in Kingskettle, Fife KY15 TJ, Scotland

*Temple Records is distributed in the United States by Rounder Records. Call (617) 354-0700 for a catalog

*Check out Steve Winick's music web site: http://www.sas.upenn.edu/~swinick

Support Arts 1000 and help maintain public funding for the arts and humanities. Call (603) 524-4511 for info.

thank you!

Grateful thanks to: B & R Heritage Enterprises; Roslyn Blyn; Myron Bretholz; Kenna Campbell; Nicholas Carolan, Glen and the pleasant people at The Traditional Music Archive, Dublin; *Les Charbonniers de l'Enfer;* Arthur Cormac; Steve Ciabottoni; Natalie Chrétien, Marie-Claude Lavoie and *La Musee de la Gaspésie;* Paul Cranford; Peter DiCecco; Helen Dunlop; Gordon and Isobel Easton; Bridgit Fitzgerald; Brendan, Deirdre, Tommy and Sheila Gunn; Joseph Hickerson and the staff of The Folklife Center at the Library of Congress; Dolores Keane and Barry Farmer; Peter and Beryl Kennedy; Ronald Labelle; James Lambert; Jill Lindsay; Tim Lyons; Jo Macdonald; Paul MacDonald; John MacInnes; Ian and Talitha MacKenzie; Seamus Mac Mathuna; Morag Macleod; Tom McKean; Robin Morton and Alison Kinnaird; Aodán O'Dubhghaill; Lisa Ornstein and the Acadian Archives/*Archives acadiennes* at the University of Maine, Ft. Kent; Michel Picard; George Pickow, Jon Pickow and Jean Ritchie; Christine Primrose; Lina Rimal; Simon Rook; everyone at the School of Scottish Studies; the Seidmann family; Laurel Sercombe; Malcolm Taylor; Carole Saulnier; Michal Shapiro; Janet Topp; Madame Bolduc-Travers; Philippe Varlet; Jesse Winch; Stephen Winick; Karen DiGesu, Maureen Gleissner, Joanna Jaeger, Sandy Saylor, Lana Wraith and the rest of the staff at Ellipsis Arts. And Candace without whom. . .

thank you!